SO YOU WANNA BE

AN ACTOR

BRITTANY CANASI

Rourke Educational Media
rourkeeducationalmedia.com

Before & After Reading Activities

Before Reading:

Building Academic Vocabulary and Background Knowledge

Before reading a book, it is important to tap into what your child or students already know about the topic. This will help them develop their vocabulary, increase their reading comprehension, and make connections across the curriculum.

1. *Look at the cover of the book. What will this book be about?*
2. *What do you already know about the topic?*
3. *Let's study the Table of Contents. What will you learn about in the book's chapters?*
4. *What would you like to learn about this topic? Do you think you might learn about it from this book? Why or why not?*
5. *Use a reading journal to write about your knowledge of this topic. Record what you already know about the topic and what you hope to learn about the topic.*
6. *Read the book.*
7. *In your reading journal, record what you learned about the topic and your response to the book.*
8. *After reading the book complete the activities below.*

Content Area Vocabulary

Read the list. What do these words mean?

adapt
auditions
commission
diaphragm
enunciation
genres
production
props
sitcoms
voiceover

After Reading:

Comprehension and Extension Activity

After reading the book, work on the following questions with your child or students in order to check their level of reading comprehension and content mastery.

1. *What does an agent do for actors? (Summarize)*
2. *Why is it important to practice a variety of acting skills? (Infer)*
3. *What types of opportunities are there for stage actors? (Asking Questions)*
4. *What types of acting appeal to you? (Text to Self Connection)*
5. *What does a voice actor do? (Asking Questions)*

Extension Activity

Research some acting classes online. Make a list of what they offer and the fees they charge. Think about some of the skills the classes focus on. Are there things you can do at home to practice these skills on your own?

TABLE OF CONTENTS

LEARNING YOUR CRAFT

Great actors know that acting takes work. They're always improving their skills and learning new ones. For instance, an actor who starts out only performing speaking parts might learn to sing or do **voiceover** work. This is where acting classes come in. Common acting classes include Shakespeare, improv, comedy, and movement.

START NOW!

Some schools offer drama classes or have after-school drama clubs. If your school doesn't, many cities have youth programs through community theaters.

Movement classes can help you become aware of how you move on stage or on camera. You can practice at home by observing an animal's movements, then imitating the way it moves and sounds.

DID YOU KNOW?!
Earning a college degree in theater doesn't mean you have to become an actor. Studying theater also teaches students excellent verbal, leadership, and problem-solving skills, and how to think under pressure.

Actors don't need college degrees. Still, majoring in theater is a good way to develop your skills and be seen. Theater students learn about stage **production** and the business side of the industry. Agents and producers sometimes attend college productions looking for new talent.

Voice coaches help actors with **enunciation** and voice strength. If an actor wants to learn to speak louder, less nasally, or more confidently, a speech coach can help. They also help with accents. Some actors want to learn an accent, and some actors want to lose their accent.

TIP!

It's important to research acting classes and coaches. Some acting classes are poorly taught, and students do not get their money's worth. Ask other actors for recommendations or research schools online before paying for classes.

Some actors hire a voice coach to expand their skills and make them more competitive in **auditions**. Some actors hire a voice coach once they've already gotten a role to help them better prepare.

WHAT'S A DEMO REEL?

After you've had some training, consider putting together a video sampling of your best voices and impressions, the characters you can play, and the range of emotions you've mastered. Demo reels can be helpful for auditions or getting representation through an agent.

theater, and cruise ship theater opportunities.

Stage actors train many ways, such as taking voice lessons, singing classes, and dance training.

A stage production cast usually includes principal actors and the ensemble. The principal actors are the main cast members. They drive the story and have the most speaking parts. The ensemble includes the supporting cast members.

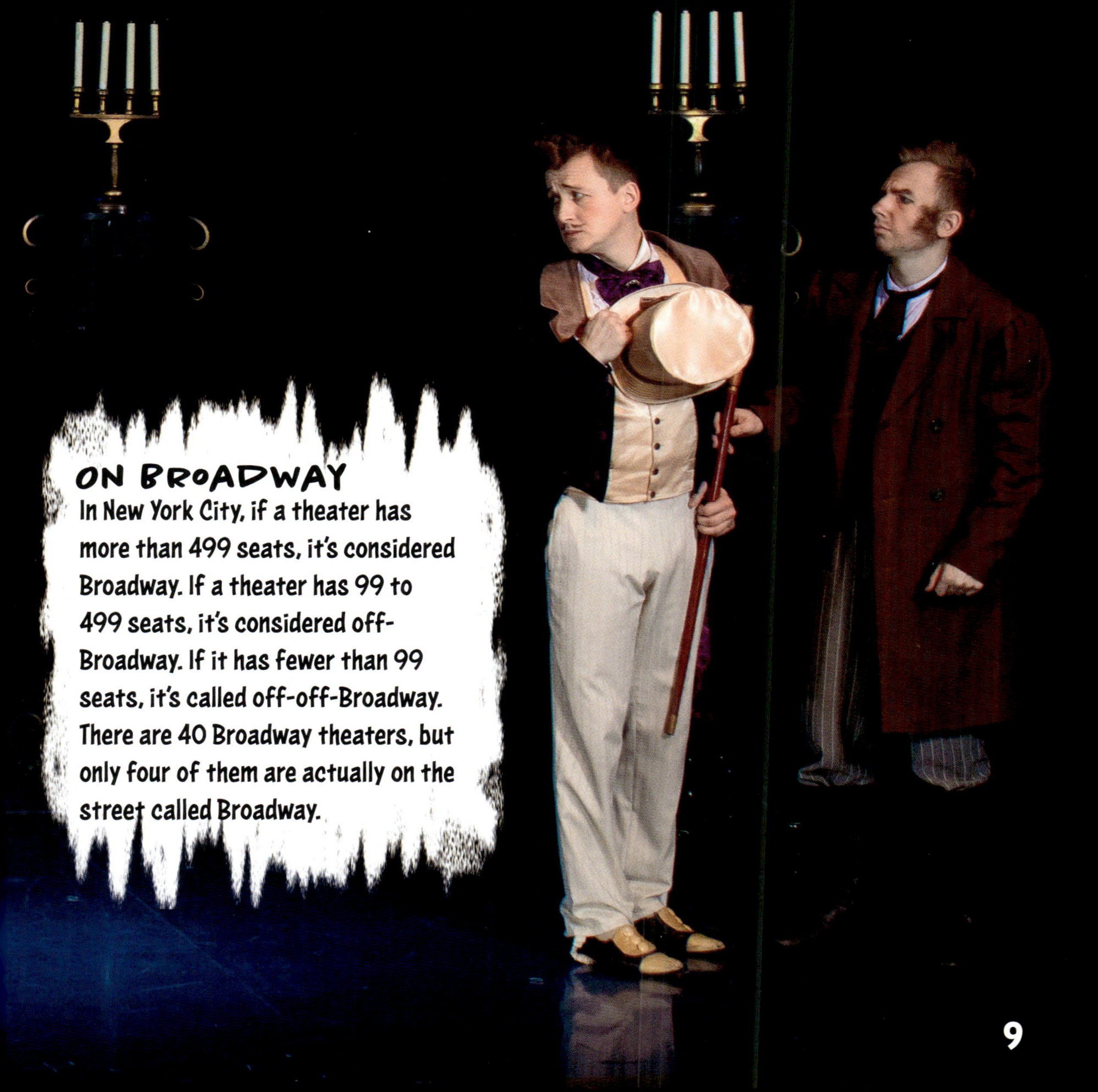

ON BROADWAY

In New York City, if a theater has more than 499 seats, it's considered Broadway. If a theater has 99 to 499 seats, it's considered off-Broadway. If it has fewer than 99 seats, it's called off-off-Broadway. There are 40 Broadway theaters, but only four of them are actually on the street called Broadway.

Stage actors who can sing, dance, and act are called "triple threats." Not all stage actors need to be triple threats. For example, an actor who can sing and/or act but not dance is called a "mover."

TIP!
If you aren't a strong dancer, your acting resume might say "moves well."

Lin Manuel-Miranda, who wrote and starred in the Broadway show ***Hamilton****, is a triple threat.*

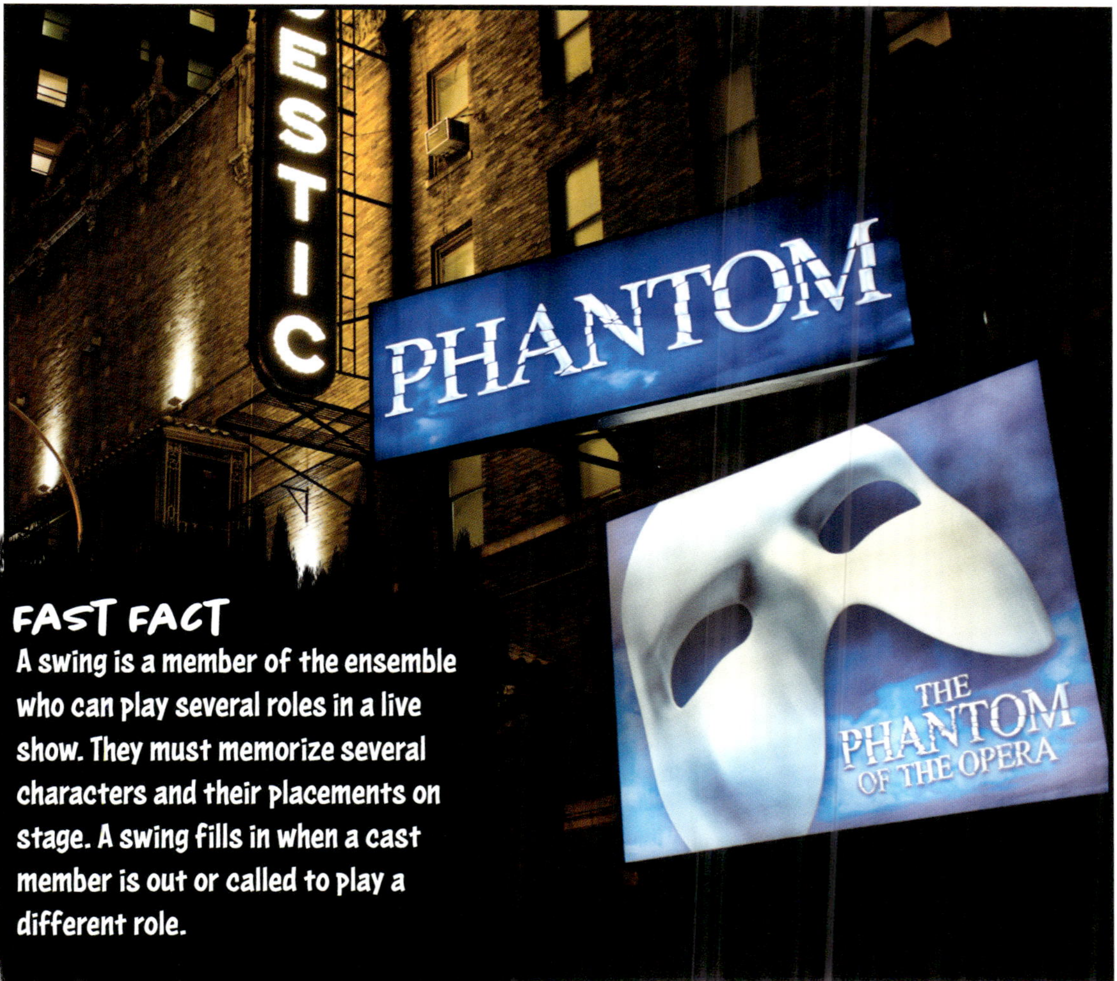

FAST FACT

A swing is a member of the ensemble who can play several roles in a live show. They must memorize several characters and their placements on stage. A swing fills in when a cast member is out or called to play a different role.

Unlike acting in television or film, a stage actor cannot **adapt** a character too much. For instance, *The Phantom of the Opera* has been performed for more than 30 years with a set script and characters. Audiences know what to expect, so the actors cannot improvise lines or put a new spin on a character.

VOICE ACTORS

Voice actors create voices for characters or provide information to an audience without appearing on-screen. Voice actors may record audiobooks, voice animated characters, or record radio advertisements, to name a few opportunities.

*Nancy Cartwright (left), voices Bart Simpson and other characters on the **The Simpsons.** Nancy poses with Matt Groening, the show's creator, Yeardley Smith, and Hank Azaria.*

Many voice actors take improv classes, which help them think on their feet. In improv, or improvisation, a story's plot and character are made up in the moment. Casting directors often ask voice actors to come up with a character or reaction on the spot. Improv classes help actors think like their characters. Rather than the actor's personal reaction to a situation, they must react the way their character would.

TRAINING YOURSELF TO BE A VOICE ACTOR

Practice reading aloud for a few minutes each day. Change your voice when you read, making up characters or doing impressions of other actors. It's also a good idea to record yourself, then play it back to hear what works and what needs improvement.

It should never sound like a voice actor is reading from a script. A voice actor performs using the same emotions and reactions as if they were on a stage or in front of a camera. Imagine if your favorite cartoon character sounded like they were always reading from a book!

SPEAKING FROM THE DIAPHRAGM

Voice lessons can help beginning voice actors learn to speak from the **diaphragm**. This makes your voice loud, clear, and free from nasally sounds. Put your hand just underneath your rib cage. Let out a deep laugh and a long yawn. Do you feel where the sound is coming from? That's your diaphragm.

From left, Walt Disney (1901 -1966) voices Mickey Mouse and Clarence Nash (1904 -1985) voices Donald Duck in a recording studio.

Voice actors should be skilled at automated dialogue replacement (ADR). ADR is when lines are recorded after a production is filmed or animated. A cartoon character may already be animated saying a sentence that hasn't yet been recorded. The voice actor will have to say the line in time with the animated lip movements. ADR also occurs in live action.

Actor Joana Santos records the voice of a video game character.

PRO ADVICE

"STUDY THEATER, BECAUSE THEATER IS THE GREATEST TRAINING GROUND THAT YOU CAN HAVE."—KEITH DAVID, SCREEN ACTOR, VOICE ACTOR, SINGER, AND COMEDIAN, IN AN INTERVIEW WITH BACKSTAGE

COMMERCIAL ACTING

There are two kinds of commercial actors: actors who become a personality, or celebrity actors who are hired to promote a product or service. Casting directors look for people who seem easily relatable and can appeal to a wide audience. Personalities are cast for commercials more than any other kind of acting. Commercials give actors the chance to create characters from scratch.

BUYER BEWARE

You should never have to pay for an audition. Once you get a job, if there are fees, such as theater group membership dues, they should be clearly listed from the start. A company should never ask you to pay for things like insurance while on set.

Audition

AUDITION TIP

An audition begins the moment the actor walks in the door. Have a great attitude and be energetic. Know how to act in front of a camera, where to look, and how to take direction.

It's helpful for commercial actors to have headshots with different looks. This shows you can play a variety of characters. For your audition, you should dress like you did in the headshot you submitted.

SCREEN ACTORS

Acting for film and television requires certain skills. A screen actor must know how to perform for a camera, which is different from performing on stage. Emotions are more visible on screen than to a stage audience. They can be performed more naturally.

Screen acting requires the ability to perform out of sequence. A film crew may shoot the last scene first, followed by the beginning scene, followed by something that takes place in the middle. An actor must know how to act in scenes that are out of order.

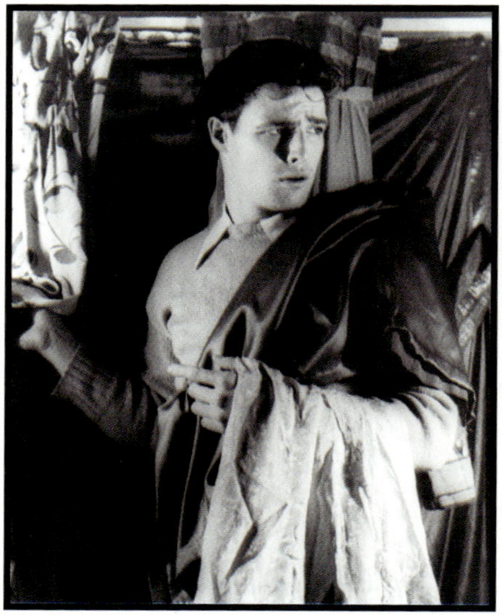

*Marlon Brando (1924 -2004) performs on the set of **A Streetcar Named Desire** (1951).*

METHOD ACTING

Method acting involves identifying completely with a character. The idea is that if an actor can feel like a character, think like a character, and fully understand the character's backstory, they will not need to act. The actor would simply be the character. Marlon Brando was a famous method actor.

PRO ADVICE

"ON-STAGE, YOU HAVE TO, IN SOME SMALL NUANCED WAY, GIVE A DEMONSTRATION OF WHAT YOU'RE THINKING SO THAT THE PEOPLE AT THE BACK CAN SEE IT, WHEREAS ON CAMERA YOU JUST QUITE LITERALLY HAVE TO THINK IT. I REALIZED THAT YOU COULD ACTUALLY HAVE A WHOLE RANGE OF THOUGHTS IN A SHORT SPACE OF TIME AND THE CAMERA WOULD SEE THEM ALL. YOU BECOME A SORT OF MENTAL GYMNAST."

—DAMIAN LEWIS, WHO TRANSITIONED FROM BEING A STAGE ACTOR TO A TELEVISION ACTOR

Screen actors must be able to do the same take over again, using the same emotions, gestures, and placement.

There are several **genres** within television and film, such as horror and thriller, adventure and action, soap operas, and **sitcoms**. Some actors will work in one genre. Others, called multi-genre actors, act across several.

LEARNING AT HOME: MOVEMENTS ON CAMERA

Watch a TV show or movie with the volume muted. Watch how the actors move and express emotions. See if you can guess what's happening in the scene.

Will Smith is a multi-genre actor.

A screen actor must know where every camera is, what the director is trying to do, and know where other actors and important **props** are. If the camera operator is trying to show an important person or object in the scene, the actors shouldn't be blocking it from view.

Some sitcoms and other TV shows are filmed in front of live audiences.

EXTRAS, UNIONS, AND AGENTS

An extra is a background actor. Some extras have speaking parts, but many do not. Working as an extra is a good way to get started in the business. Most extras just need a headshot and proof they can legally work.

Extras often work long days. Some shoots require extras to be on set for up to 12 hours. Extras on music video sets could be required on set for up to 16 hours. It is important to remember direction and do the exact same thing with each take.

*Extras fill the deck of a ship on the set of **Dunkirk** (2017).*

GET ON THE LIST

To learn about extras job opportunities, contact an extras casting director and ask to be put on their list. Many of these lists are free, but some may charge a small fee to file paperwork. This is normal. Be skeptical if one of these services charges a lot of money for their list or tries to sell headshots or acting classes.

SAG-AFTRA is a union that supports actors. The union can provide training, help actors get roles, and help with insurance and retirement options.

Unions offer collective bargaining. This means they help get better options for people by negotiating for its members as a team, rather than for individuals.

DID YOU KNOW?!

SAG, or Screen Actors Guild, started in 1933 for film and television actors. AFTRA, or American Federation of Television and Radio Actors, started in 1937 for television and radio actors, as well as singers and stunt performers. They merged in 2012 to become SAG-AFTRA.

SAG-AFTRA represents about 160,000 screen actors, singers, radio personalities, journalists, recording artists, and other professionals.

Screen actors cast in main roles in TV or film can join the union. Other actors not in main roles must work as a SAG extra for three days before they can join. Every production must hire a certain number of union extras, and the rest can be non-union. If a non-union extra does not show up, the assistant director will give a union voucher to a non-union extra. The voucher is equal to one day's work.

GET NOTICED

It is usually up to the assistant director who gets an available union voucher. Get their attention by showing up early, being courteous and professional, and volunteering to help if it's needed.

A talent agent finds jobs for actors. They also negotiate deals for their clients. Agents have access to casting calls that are not always open to the public.

An agent is paid when an actor makes money. They usually get a 10 percent **commission** from the actor's earnings.

WHAT'S A MANAGER?

A manager takes on fewer clients than an agent, so they can spend more time with each client. Agents are regulated by state laws, but managers are not. Some actors have a manager and an agent. Managers can't negotiate contracts like agents. If an actor only has a manager, they can hire a lawyer to negotiate contracts.

Talent agent Dolores Dioguardi represented actor Tom Cruise at the beginning of his career.

ACTING AS A HOBBY

If you like acting but don't want to do it professionally, you can always enjoy it as a hobby! While most acting jobs in the United States are in Los Angeles or New York, if you're just performing for fun, you can live anywhere.

COMMUNITY THEATER

Community theater companies exist all over. They can be a mix of professionals, non-professionals who have experience in acting, and people who have never acted but would like to learn. See if your hometown has a community theater group by searching online. Want help starting your own? The American Association of Community Theater is a great resource.

Pursuing acting as a hobby doesn't mean you can't go on auditions with career actors. Many television shows and films shoot in cities all over. They always need local background actors. The experience you gain can help you if you decide to pursue acting as a career in the future.

GLOSSARY

adapt (uh-DAPT): to make something work in a different way or for a different purpose

auditions (aw-DISH-uhns): small performances by an actor, singer, musician, or dancer to see whether he or she is suitable for a part in a play, concert, or other performance

commission (kuh-MISH-uhn): an amount of money paid to an agent in a business transaction

diaphragm (DYE-uh-fram): the wall of muscle in your lower chest that draws air into and pushes air out of your lungs

enunciation (i-nuhn-see-AY-shun): speaking or pronouncing words

genres (ZHAHN-ruhs): particular kinds of creative work

production (pruh-DUHK-shuhn): any form of entertainment that is presented to others

props (prahps): any items other than costumes or furniture that appears on a stage or movie set

sitcoms (SIT-kahms): humorous television programs that feature the same group of characters each week

voiceover (VOIS-oh-vur): the voice of an off-screen narrator or announcer

INDEX

SHOW WHAT YOU KNOW

1. What is the name for supporting cast members in a stage play?
2. How do agents make their money?
3. Why are different headshots important for commercial auditions?
4. What is a manager not able to do for their client?
5. Why are voice coaches important?

FURTHER READING

Armstrong, Linda J., *African Americans in Radio, Film, and TV Entertainment*, Simon & Schuster, 2014.

Kruse, Jeremy, *The Young Actor's Handbook*, Applause Theater & Cinema Books, 2017.

Wood, Alix, *Be an Actor*, Rosen Publishing, 2018.

ABOUT THE AUTHOR

Brittany Canasi's job is in cartoons, and her passion is in writing. She's worked in the entertainment industry for nearly a decade and has a B.A. in Creative Writing from Florida State University. Her favorite part of working in cartoons is watching voice actors come up with new characters on the spot. She lives in Los Angeles with her husband and very scruffy dogs.

Meet The Author!
www.meetREMauthors.com

www.rourkeeducationalmedia.com

PHOTO CREDITS: Cover & Title Pg ©serts, ©Bet_Noire, Background ©Nasared, Pg 15 & 19 ©MariatKary, Pg 4 ©Highwaystarz-Photography, Pg 5 ©ferrantraite, Pg 6 ©By Lisa F. Young, Pg 7 ©Mordolff, Pg 8 ©Kozlik, Pg 10 ©ZUMA Press, Inc./Alamy Stock Photo, Pg 11 ©aluxum, Pg 12 ©Jaguar/Alamy Stock Photo, Pg 13 ©Monkeybusinessimages, Pg 14 ©RBM Vintage Images/Alamy Stock Photo, Pg 15 ©G0r3cki, ©By Kathy Hutchins, Pg 16 ©JoKMedia, Pg 17 ©DeluXe-PiX, ©By Veronica Louro, Pg 18 ©Library of Congress, Pg 19 ©guruXOOX, ©By JStone, Pg 20 ©By Andrey Bayda, Pg 21 ©By Pavel L Photo and Video, Pg 23 ©By fokke baarssen, Pg 24 ©By Kathy Hutchins, Pg 25 ©By LunaseeStudios, Pg 26 ©By LeoWolfert, Pg 27 ©ZUMA Press Inc/Alamy Stock Photo, Pg 28 ©CREATISTA, Pg 29 ©Wavebreakmedia,

Edited by: Keli Sipperley
Cover and Interior design by: Rhea Magaro-Wallace

Library of Congress PCN Data

An Actor / Brittany Canasi
(So You Wanna Be)
ISBN 978-1-64156-469-4 (hard cover)
ISBN 978-1-64156-595-0 (soft cover)
ISBN 978-1-64156-710-7 (e-Book)
Library of Congress Control Number: 2018930505

Rourke Educational Media
Printed in the United States of America,
North Mankato, Minnesota